God *is*

REAL

The Eyewitness Testimony

of a Former Atheist

Kim Endraske

"Even die-hard atheists are not beyond the reach of God's grace. Here is the story of a young woman who was proud to be living on her terms in a world without God. But at the same time, God was ordering circumstances and using her husband (even before he became her husband) to rescue her from herself. She didn't stand a chance against the love of God.

Her story shouts to us all, "Don't write anyone off, no matter how deep her defiance of the truth. Keep showing her (or him) the love of Jesus and give them the gospel. To do so is not in vain."

Don't believe me? Want proof? Keep reading Kim Endraske's story."

- Pastor Jim Fleming

ISBN: 978-1-975916329

*"Now Thomas, one of the Twelve, called the Twin, was not with them when Jesus came. So the other disciples told him, "We have seen the Lord." But he said to them, "Unless I see in his hands the mark of the nails, and place my finger into the mark of the nails, and place my hand into his side, **I will never believe**."*

Eight days later, his disciples were inside again, and Thomas was with them. Although the doors were locked, Jesus came and stood among them and said, "Peace be with you."

Then he said to Thomas, "Put your finger here, and see my hands; and put out your hand, and place it in my side. Do not disbelieve, but believe."

*Thomas answered him, **"My Lord and my God!"***

Jesus said to him, "Have you believed because you have seen me? Blessed are those who have not seen and yet have believed."

Now Jesus did many other signs in the presence of the disciples, which are not written in this book; but these are written so that you may believe that Jesus is the Christ, the Son of God, and that by believing you may have life in his name."

John 20:24-31

Contents

Welcome

Twenty-five years ago, when I was a young adult shouting the praises of atheism, I heard very few echoes in reply. This is no longer the case. Allen Downey, in an article for *Scientific American*, wrote, "The number of college students with no religious affiliation has tripled in the last 30 years, from 10 percent in 1986 to 31 percent in 2016, according to data from the CIRP Freshman Survey."[1]

This is the landscape of not only college campuses. Rather, according to the 2014 U.S. Religious Landscape Study conducted by the Pew Research Center, "Nearly one-in-ten U.S. adults overall (9%) now say they do not believe in God, up from 5% in 2007." [2] "Older generations of American adults who were overwhelmingly Christian by affiliation and comparatively devout in belief and behavior are gradually passing away. They are being replaced by a new generation of young people who are, on the whole, less inclined to identify with any branch of

Christianity and more religiously unaffiliated than older cohorts ever were, even when they were young." [3]

Maybe you're currently an atheist, but are skeptical (or curious) of how a fellow atheist came to faith in the God of the Bible. Maybe you have a loved one who is an atheist and you're wondering how to reach out to them. Or maybe you're a Christian struggling in your own faith and looking for encouragement to believe.

No matter what your religious leanings, you are welcome here. I am glad you've come. This is not your standard introduction where I tell you about myself, because you'll get plenty of that in the pages of this book. Rather, this is an invitation to come in and get to know me better and get to know God better as you see Him at work in one woman's life.

This is also an invitation to dive deeper by actively responding to what you read, studying the referenced Scripture passages (which can be found at the end of this book), and jotting down your replies in the "A Time to Reflect" sections that appear at the end of each chapter. The chapters are intentionally short to make it easier to read together with a group. Please consider inviting some of your friends, family members or neighbors to join you to read and discuss it together.

I'm praying for you. May you see the God who never changes, the God who is the same yesterday, today and forever at work in the Scriptures, in my life, and in yours. May you see how my life story relates to your own life experiences and catch the vision to pass on your own stories of God's faithfulness. I pray that you will "believe that Jesus is the Christ, the Son of God, and that by believing you may have life in his name" (John 20:31). Now, please join me, as I walk you through my own eyewitness account of how Jesus transformed me from an evangelical atheist to an evangelical Christian.

---

[1] "Data From a Nationwide Survey Shows Students Who List Their Affiliation as "None" has Skyrocketed." Scientific American, (May 25, 2017). https://blogs.scientificamerican.com/observations/college-freshmen-are-less-religious-than-ever/
[2] "U.S. Public Becoming Less Religious." Pew Research Center, (Nov. 1, 2015). https://pewforum.org/2015/11/03/u-s-public-becoming-less-religious/
[3] Ibid

"I thank him who has given me strength, Christ Jesus our Lord, because he judged me faithful, appointing me to his service, though formerly I was a blasphemer, persecutor, and insolent opponent. But I received mercy because I had acted ignorantly in unbelief, and the grace of our Lord overflowed for me with the faith and love that are in Christ Jesus.

The saying is trustworthy and deserving of full acceptance, that Christ Jesus came into the world to save sinners, of whom I am the foremost. But I received mercy for this reason, that in me, as the foremost, Jesus Christ might display his perfect patience as an example to those who were to believe in him for eternal life."

1 Timothy 1:12-16

Girl Meets Boy

A latch-key kid from my earliest memories, I leaned my head against the cold metal window frame of my long yellow school bus, sleep shutting out the noise of my fellow passengers. After trekking the half-mile walk home, and stretching out on our living room couch to read one of the dozen books I'd checked out at the library, sleep once again enveloped me before my parents arrived home from work. If the weather had been nice, I would've chosen instead to climb the massive mulberry tree in our backyard to watch highway traffic zoom by behind our Des Moines, Iowa, home.

With one sister three years my senior, sibling rivalry was an underlying theme of my daily life. My poor mother fielded my pitiful phone calls, listening somewhat patiently to my slightly-exaggerated stories of Kristan's latest mean tricks. On happier occasions, Kristan and I played kickball together with a handful of our neighbors in our front yard or concocted fanciful recipes in our well-stocked kitchen or tossed the frisbee by streetlights well into the evening hours. By the time I entered high school, our constant rivalry finally came to an end and my sister and I became close friends and confidants.

Though by no means a devout church-going family, my parents certainly expected us to be kind and good. They trained their children to be independent thinkers and we were given great freedom to make our own choices. Academic

excellence was expected, and we were consistently encouraged to do our best. My parents were motivated by doing what they thought was right, even though as far as I could tell our whole family was just making up our own rules.

Early on I discovered that I liked making up rules for myself - and for others. I liked making up rules that I wanted to follow, while feeling free to change them as life went on. Obeying these rules helped me to feel good about myself and fueled my ever-growing pride.

A bright student, I excelled at school (except in handwriting and gym class). In fourth grade, I scored a perfect score on the state's standardized achievement test and was promoted mid-year to fifth grade. Branded with a big "N" for nerd across my chest, and rejected by my friends, I floundered to find my place in the school social life.

Thankfully, in eighth grade, I began attending a brand-new magnet school for talented and gifted students. In this safe environment, I thrived. Suddenly earning a top spot in the popularity ranks with my outgoing spirit and quick wit, I discovered the excitement of winning the attention of boys, going from one boyfriend to another without too much discernment into their character. It seemed that my only prerequisite for dating was for them to be interested in me.

By high school, my disdain for faith in any kind of higher power had grown into my own self-titled term, "evangelical atheist." I got a rush out of making the Christians I met look and feel foolish. Today atheism has become relatively socially acceptable, even cool, especially on college campuses. But not back then. When I declared to my latest unsuspecting victim that I was an atheist, I was met with a blank stare. At my high school, drawing the most academically gifted from five local high schools, there were a few who shared my skeptical viewpoint, but we were the still a minority.

Receiving a full academic scholarship to attend a small college in Illinois, I looked forward to changing the world as a teacher, majoring in "Education of the Hearing Impaired" with a minor in English. That very first semester of school, I met a popular football jock and we soon started dating. Our relationship was unhealthy to say the least. He wasn't good for me and, honestly, I wasn't good for him, either. Neither of us knew how to resolve conflict ... and we had plenty of conflict.

The summer before our senior year, I accepted his proposal, hours after being slapped across the face in a sudden burst of anger. Believing his promises to change, and trusting in my abilities to reform him, we began planning a wedding for just after our upcoming graduation. Eagerly, I bought a simple white off-the-shoulder wedding gown and ordered the necessary wedding invitations which came to rest in the corner of my concrete-block-walled dorm room.

In my last quarter of school before graduating, I was offered the opportunity to student teach in St. Louis, a couple of hours away. My parents were about to celebrate their 25th wedding anniversary and I sincerely believed that marriage was "'til death do we part." I was finally waking up to the realities of spending a lifetime with this angry man and I saw this opportunity as my chance to get away. Abruptly I broke off the engagement and headed for a new town, hoping the distance would give me a clean slate and make the break-up easier.

Just weeks after moving to St. Louis, I received an unexpected call from my friend, Kirsten, who I'd known in college, but had lost touch with a year earlier. She had asked her mom to track me down because I hadn't responded to the wedding invitation she had mailed out a month prior. (In fact, I had intentionally not replied as I had absolutely no interest in attending her wedding.) Over the phone, Kirsten insisted that I just *had* to come to her wedding.

"When is it?" I asked.

"Tomorrow," she replied, tentatively.

What bride tracks down long-lost friends the day before her wedding to make sure they've received the wedding invitation? This was certainly odd!

Odd, yes, but not as odd as this: I was an Iowa-born, Illinois-college attending young woman who was living for two months in St. Louis and I was being invited to a wedding taking place in the great city of St. Louis itself.

I simply couldn't think of any good reason not to go, so the next day I half-heartedly attended her wedding, and that decision changed the course of my life. That afternoon, I met Bill, the man that God would use to share His love with me.

Meanwhile, Bill had a story brewing all of his own. Every New Year's Eve his family hosted a grand get-together with a dozen other families. At this party, everyone wrote down their prayers for the new year, which would be tucked away in a large manila envelope waiting for the following New Year's Eve to be shared. Bill had prayed for a car, a job and a girlfriend.

Four months later, Bill got his first car (a sporty red one that attracted my attention immediately when he pulled around the corner at my friend's wedding), his first job (walking distance from where I was student teaching), and his first "real" girlfriend.

A Time to Reflect

- What have you prayed for recently? Have you received it?

- Do you tend to be a rule maker or a rule breaker? How and why?

- Read Acts 8:26-40 in the Bible (or in the back of this book). This is the story of Philip sharing the good news of Jesus with the eunuch from Ethiopia. Reflect on how God worked to bring Philip to this seeking man. Write out the verses you'd like to remember.

- In your lifetime, has anyone shared the good news about Jesus with you? What events led up to that moment? In what ways did they help you to understand what you'd been unable to understand before?

Encountering Jesus

As far back as I can remember, I didn't believe in any kind of supernatural being or life after death. My mother has repeatedly told the story of her shock at overhearing me announce to my grandmother that there was no god. I was in kindergarten. What kindergartener says such a thing?

I don't recall my parents ever specifically talking with me about the existence or non-existence of God, but from what I could tell our family lived our lives on our own terms, free from any religious underpinnings. One evening, while sitting at dinner in a fast food restaurant with my mom, I asked her why we didn't go to church. She explained to me that though she and my dad had been raised in religious homes, they did not want to indoctrinate us into the Christian faith, preferring instead for us to make our own decisions when we were ready. Then, my mom shared that when my sister was born, her pastor had insisted that she needed to have the baby baptized. In response to that demand, my parents made a break from regular church attendance. To this day, there is still disagreement between my parents as to whether my sister was or was not baptized. (They do agree, by the way, that I wasn't.)

I do still admire my parents for raising their children to be independent thinkers. They taught us to question and research and seek the truth. Yet, as flawed people like the rest of us, they did not recognize the fact that all children model their lives after their parents. Largely as a result of observing my parents' lack of faith, as well as the lack of any consistent religious input from my extended family or community, I became an atheistic humanist. This was not primarily an intellectually rational decision made after months and years of diligent study. Rather, it was my default position, the natural result of the void of God in my world.

My atheistic views became stronger and more passionate as I aged because of my disgust with many of the professing Christians I met. Recurrent immorality, an inability to defend their beliefs, and their failure to be able to explain what they believed and why, caused me to doubt all the more the God they proclaimed. If Christianity was true, why were its followers so wishy-washy and phony?

During these formative years, I had a handful of interactions with Christians that helped shape my views on Christianity, many for good and many more for bad. I admired the few Christians I met who took a bold stand for their faith, like an older gentleman in a shabby jacket who wordlessly presented me with an orange-covered pocket-sized Bible as I walked home from middle school one chilly day. I respected a quiet boy I liked in high school who insisted that we couldn't date because he could never marry me, since I "wouldn't be in heaven."

One day in high school, an acquaintance invited me to attend youth group with her. My honest reply was, "What's youth group?" When she told me that it was when teenagers from her church got together to hang out and talk, I wondered why I would want to do *that*.

On another occasion this same friend was laughing with a fellow youth group member about them being "holy rollers" and something else I didn't understand about "holy laughter." I'm sure the confused look on my face baffled her. I was such a know-it-all smarty pants, that I think they expected me to know all about church stuff. But, I didn't. Rather than taking my confusion seriously, they made me feel even more foolish at my lack of understanding.

One school day, during physics class, I began privately discussing evolution with a bright girl I liked who I knew was a Christian. Her explanation to me that God had intentionally placed fossils in the earth to test our faith sounded so absurd and cruel, that I all the more strongly doubted creationism. The theory of evolution had been taught to me so consistently my entire life both at home and at school that believing in a God who created the universe seemed ridiculous. No one, including this young friend, ever explained to me that there were scientific reasons to doubt evolution and to believe in the Biblical account of creation. (For more on this, please see the "Recommended Resources" list in the back of this book.)

I saw Christians as hypocrites, liars and foolish sheep just following the pack. It felt like I made them uncomfortable and irritated, and that their primary goal in reaching out to me was to get me "cleaned up." It seemed like they'd be happy if they could get me to quit cussing, wearing mini skirts and sleeping with my boyfriend. This was made even more ironic, since so many of them were cussing, wearing mini skirts and sleeping with their boyfriends, too. I thought Christianity was a list of do's and don'ts, and rules to follow, rather than about a living relationship with a living God flowing out of a spirit of faith.

In college I had several classes where we studied world religions, including Christianity, Judaism and Islam. We read the story of Job from the Bible as a great work of ancient literature. I memorized the definition of transsubstantiation and the five pillars of Islam, but somehow missed out on the meaning of the "gospel."

In all honesty, I didn't think too much about God's existence on a regular basis, except when the opportunity arose to argue about how foolish it was to believe in one. There were, though, two diametrically opposed topics that caused me to consider the presence of the supernatural: *death* and *beauty*. Death, because, well, it scared me to death (pun intended). Beauty, because it forced me to question my firm faith in evolution.

Chiefly because of my disbelief in any kind of afterlife, I lived in fear of dying. The first time I can recall seriously thinking about whether God was real was when I was about eight or nine years old. That summer I was spending a week with my grandmother who lived out of town. While lying in bed one night, trying to fall asleep and listening to her breathing peacefully next to me, I began to think about death, imagining being laid in an empty grave. Picturing an enormous black void, my heart was filled with fear.

This fear fed even more my addiction to making rules. I wore my seatbelt and insisted that the rest of my family wear theirs. On multiple occasions, I flushed my parents' cigarettes down the toilet and left them passionately written notes urging them to quit smoking. I even went so far as making them a pottery ashtray with something like, "Don't Use This," scrawled in the bottom of the bowl. I didn't smoke, drink or do drugs, partially because I thought it was "wrong," but even more so because I was afraid of shortening my life.

Don't be fooled, though, I was plenty immoral in a whole variety of other ways. I was a selfish, lying, prideful manipulator who you better not cross. No one wanted to meet the "wrath of Kim." Those things, though, did not put me in danger of dying!

On the opposite end of the spectrum there was the simple

existence of beauty. Beautiful things made me think about creation and, therefore, about God. I struggled to reconcile the existence of amazing beauty and order in the world and my belief that the world came into being by random chance.

When I finished my sophomore year of high school, I flew out to Vermont for two weeks of summer debate camp. One afternoon while sitting alone in a vast, green field, the sun beating on my face and the breeze blowing gently, I gazed up into the immense blue sky and thought, "God, if You are real, please show Yourself to me." Hearing no audible voice in response, I stuffed those thoughts back into the remote crevices of my mind and pressed forward in my ever-growing faith in atheism.

But the truth is, God *was* indeed showing Himself to me, though I didn't recognize it at the time. God has revealed Himself to all of creation in the things that He has made. In the Bible, we are told that God's, "invisible attributes, namely, his eternal power and divine nature, have been clearly perceived, ever since the creation of the world, in the things that have been made. So they are without excuse." (Romans 1:20)

That particular afternoon was just one of many times when I looked with wonder at the beauty of the world, whether the enormity of the ocean, the incredible heights of the snow-capped Rocky Mountains, or the intricate formation of a newborn baby, and marveled at how these things could have come into existence without God.

Believing that all of this beauty had come about through a series of random events over millions and millions of years, caused my own life to lack hope and value. If my life was nothing more than the natural result of billions of accidental, chance occurrences, what was the purpose in living?

When I met Bill at my friend's wedding, my primary goal was to get him interested in me ... but after hearing about his religious beliefs, a close second was to convert him to atheism. I wanted him to see the foolishness of believing in anything supernatural. I couldn't imagine that any intelligent person would believe that the Bible was literally the Word of God. I scoffed at any arguments he made that were based on Christian scriptures.

In the weeks after meeting, we had many late-night conversations (or more accurately, debates) about God. This young man had grown up in a Christian home and he made it clear to me that he could never get serious with someone who wasn't a Christian themselves. He cared about me from that very first day we met, despite my obvious brokenness. He managed to look past my glaring external sins, seeing my genuine need for a

Savior, and he refused to turn his back on me when I put up my defenses.

One night, Bill made some off-hand comment about a person being "saved." In a rare moment of humility, I confessed that I didn't know what that meant. It was a word he'd casually tossed out several times, but he might as well have been speaking Mandarin Chinese. In my way of thinking, people "save" money. People "save" abandoned puppies. Why did a person need to be saved? What did I need to be saved from?

And for the first time in my life I heard the gospel, the good news of Jesus, the Savior of the World, God in human flesh. It still brings tears to my eyes to remember that moment.

I was 21 years old. I'd grown up in the Midwest. I'd attended church at least a dozen times with my grandparents. I'd graduated the valedictorian of a small college sponsored by a Christian denomination. And yet, as hard as it may be to believe, I had never understood that Jesus claimed to be God in the flesh. I didn't realize that Jesus had died on the cross to pay the punishment for man's sin. I didn't know the children's song, "Jesus Loves Me" nor did I know that Jesus indeed loved me.

Despite my top ACT score, I was unfamiliar with even basic Bible stories, like Daniel's protection in the lion's den, or David's amazing defeat of the giant, Goliath. I had no recollection of ever hearing the famous Bible verse, John 3:16,

"For God so loved the world, that he gave his only Son, that whoever believes in him should not perish but have eternal life." In fact, when Bill told me to look in the book of John, I didn't realize that "John" was *in* the Bible – I thought it was some kind of a separate book.

For the first time in my memory, I heard that I was a sinner; that Jesus' death had paid the penalty for my sins; and that through faith in Him, I could be set free from my slavery to sin, receive forgiveness, and enjoy everlasting life. My life could finally have the meaning and purpose I so desperately needed, the meaning and purpose that all of mankind was created to need. And that very night, with faith the size of a mustard seed, I asked the God of the universe to forgive me of my sins. I acknowledged Jesus as my Savior and King, and my life has never been the same. I prayed, "God, I want to believe in You. If You are real, please change my heart. Please forgive me for all my years of running from You and denying You. Please save me and be my King."

It's been almost twenty-five years now, but the trajectory of my life changed that night. Without any conscious effort on my own part, my entire value system began to change. Once an evangelical atheist, I suddenly became an evangelical (though ill-prepared) Christian. Most dramatically, I was now able to understand and believe what I read in the Bible. What had once seemed pure insanity, was now pure inspiration.

If this is all new to you, please, would you pray and seek the

Lord for yourself? Read the Bible, particularly the New Testament books of John and Romans. (You'll find them in the second half of the Bible.) Read a few of the "Recommended Resources" from the list in the back of this book. Get involved in a Bible-believing church. Ask questions.

The Lord is indeed *real* and He does so *many* unimaginable, unexplainable things, particularly giving new birth to His children. You can email me directly at formeratheist58@gmail.com. I'd love to hear from you.

A Time to Reflect

- What experiences have you had (for good or bad) with Christians? With atheists?

- What do you think it means to be "saved?"

- Read Acts 9:1-22 in the Bible (or in the back of this book). This is the story of Saul meeting Jesus. Reflect on how Saul was dramatically transformed by this encounter. Write out the verses you'd like to remember.

- How have you searched for God? What have you found?

- Have you surrendered your life to Jesus? If not, what obstacles are standing in your way? If so, what circumstances surrounded your new birth as a follower of Jesus?

The Battle

I have learned that there is a vast difference between believing that God is real, and submitting your life to Him as your sovereign King. Most of the people in our great nation are not atheists. They believe in "God." But they have not placed themselves under God's control. God is not on the throne of their lives. They are still living according to their own rules.

For me, as soon as I accepted that God was real, I recognized that He was supposed to be my boss. But, obeying Him was *not* as easy as I expected. As the Holy Spirit took up residence in my soul, I was stunned by the daily battles I was fighting. There was a tug-of-war in my heart between the forces of good and evil for which I was unprepared. I thought that once I believed in God, then I would suddenly be perfect. Nope. I still struggled to be kind. I still struggled to tell the truth. I still struggled to serve others instead of myself.

Just a few months after becoming a follower of Jesus Christ, Bill and I were engaged. Six months later, we were married. I brought into my marriage loads of baggage from my 3½ year long relationship with my ex-fiancé that had been riddled with extreme episodes of anger. I had a difficult time fully investing in my marriage and I struggled to trust my new husband after being so badly hurt. Bill was a good husband. He was a gentle man. He wasn't really doing anything *wrong*. But I missed the adrenaline and passion associated with the high levels of energy and emotion to which I was accustomed. I missed being able to say whatever I wanted, whenever I wanted. I missed making up after a big fight. I missed the extreme transparency that I had shared with my ex.

A few months after getting married, I snuck upstairs to call my ex-fiancé. In the quiet of a dark attic room, I poured out my heart over a long-distance phone call. In spite of all the mess of our past, he had been my closest friend for over three years of my life. I could talk to him about anything. The conversation accomplished nothing, except to confirm for me that our relationship was seriously messed up.

I felt terribly guilty about this emotional infidelity and within a few days, I confessed to Bill what I had done, hoping that he would see the pain I was in, and be motivated to be more open with me. Rather, in pouring out my sin and pain to him, Bill felt all the more inadequate and withdrew even farther from me.

Right in the middle of this dreadful battle, though, was a new experience: forgiveness. Real forgiveness. The cleansing love of Christ poured into my broken heart, reaching deep into my soul and performing some much-needed housekeeping. When I ached for the comfort of the past, Jesus extended His arms of love to rescue me.

His mercy and grace were healing me in a way that I'd never before encountered. Gradually, I began to understand that I could to go to God with my sin and pain. And this made me love Jesus even more than I ever thought possible. It still brings tears to my eyes.

I was overwhelmed by His goodness. I wanted to tell everyone I knew about Jesus. I wanted everyone to know what it meant to be "saved." The first people I told were my sister and my parents. They were happy to hear that I'd found something that made me happy. But, I wanted more than that. I wanted desperately for them to experience the joy and hope and love and purpose and light that I was experiencing.

No longer was my evangelism motivated by selfishness. Now I genuinely wanted for the other person's good, rather than wanting to show off my own smarts. Yet my evangelism tools remained largely the same. I was still debating, arguing, pushing and shaming my opponent. I was still trying to *win*. I had not yet learned the wisdom found in 2 Timothy 2:24-25a, that "the Lord's servant must not be quarrelsome but kind to everyone, able to teach, patiently enduring evil, correcting his opponents with gentleness."

I had become a believer in Jesus as the Son of God and Savior of my life, and truly was a new creation in Christ, but I still knew next to nothing about the Bible. Unfortunately, after sharing the gospel with me, Bill had not continued to disciple me beyond encouraging me to go to church and to pray. I'd been thrown a life-preserver so I was no longer drowning (Thank You, Jesus!), but I had no idea how to reach the safety of the solid shore. The sermons at church were so far over my head that I wasn't getting much out of them. The songs were all foreign to me, and I had no idea how to pray on my own. I desperately needed some female accountability and discipleship, but my pride kept other women at arm's length.

After almost ten years, I still had not been able to fully sever my emotional ties to my ex-fiancé. Though the battlefield looked slightly different, I was still being haunted by "the ghost of boyfriend past." One day I finally opened up to a small group of ladies who I'd begun meeting with weekly. Sharing with them the stronghold my ex-fiancé still had over my life, I asked them to pray for me and for my marriage.

And in God's perfect, providential timing, the very next day the alumni department of my college called me with a message from my ex. He wanted to reconnect. He'd contacted them, looking for my phone number. This was the first time I'd heard from him since he'd sent me an autographed bodybuilding magazine with him on the cover some eight years earlier.

This time around, though, I checked with my husband *first*.

I asked for his permission to return his call, and he gave it to me. This conversation was very different from the secret conversation we'd had ten years earlier. My purpose was altogether different this time around. This time, I was not motivated to meet my own needs, but to minister to his. This time, I shared with him the joy that I had found in the arms of Jesus. Through tears, I shared with him how he, too, could find peace and forgiveness.

But he wasn't ready. He was still going his own way and was just hoping that I'd join up with him on his path. But that's not who I was anymore. The old was gone and the new had come. Blessed be the name of the Lord, indeed.

I had not only found forgiveness for myself, but I'd finally been able to give forgiveness to the man who had wreaked havoc on my heart. I finally had the strength to say, "Forgive him, Father, for he knew not what he was doing." And that day I was set free from the captivity that unforgiveness had held me in for all those years.

A Time to Reflect

- Who are you struggling to forgive right now?

- Read Luke 7:36-50 in the Bible (or in the back of this book). This is the story of the sinful woman being forgiven. Reflect on the depth of her love for Jesus. Write out the verses you'd like to remember.

- How have you had to battle to leave the sins of your past?

- How has the forgiveness of Jesus impacted or changed you?

- Who is God calling you to share His love and forgiveness with today?

Blessed

After being married a scant six months, two blue lines appeared on the pregnancy test I'd picked up at the local drug store. I was pregnant, and thrilled. (And nervous.) Only one month later, though, I began bleeding. Our first baby, smaller than the size of my own thumb, was delivered silently in the white-tiled bathroom of our brick bungalow.

My older sister, Kristan, had suffered two miscarriages herself earlier that year and was now pregnant for a third time. I feared the worst. I grieved the loss of our much wanted child, yet even more greatly, I grieved the idea of never holding a living child in my arms.

Despite my doctor's advice to wait three months before trying to conceive, I found myself pregnant again the very next month! To our great joy, the Lord blessed us with month after month of healthy ultrasounds as our new little one grew and grew. And on April 18, 1996, born exactly one-month early, our beautiful baby girl, Emily Elizabeth Endraske made her entrance into the world.

My sister's third pregnancy resulted in a bundle of love named Brady. Brady was born just three months before our daughter, Emily. Kristan and her husband, Chad, made their home in rural Colorado, having recently moved to a 300-acre ranch to raise elk.

For Valentine's Day, I sent my sister a Bible. Five years earlier, she had graduated from college with a degree in

philosophy. After seeing the transformation in my own life and having many passionate discussions about the existence of God and the truth of the Scriptures, she was genuinely evaluating her own lack of faith in God. Kristan was not an outspoken atheist like I had been. She preferred to use the term, "agnostic." At my encouragement, she started reading several Christian apologetics books, including Evidence that Demands a Verdict by Josh McDowell, and she began to tentatively read through the Bible.

On May 4, 1997, when Brady was sixteen months old, Kristan delivered a second son. She and Chad chose to name him Matthew, because it meant "gift from God." I confess I was surprised by this choice, since Kristan was still questioning God's existence. Yet I could see God at work in drawing her closer to faith in Him.

The day after Matthew was born, the excited family of four returned home from the hospital. Hours later, my mom called me, her voice shaking, and I feared that something had happened to newborn Matthew. I was wrong.

Mom had been helping Kristan sort through Brady's outgrown baby clothes, preparing to pass them on to his new baby brother. Brady had ventured out with his dad and grandpa to go work on a windmill, when in a split-second our lives were forever changed. My one-year-old nephew was accidentally run over as Chad pulled his truck out of the shop. Blond-haired, blue-eyed Brady died in his mother's arms as she frantically attempted CPR, waiting for an ambulance to arrive.

As indescribably painful as this story is to put down on paper, and as difficult as it must be to read these words, I know without a doubt that precious one-day-old Matthew truly was a gift from God, in more ways than any human being can possibly comprehend.

This newborn baby boy forced Kristan to keep going when everything in her and her husband wanted to just curl up in bed and never get up. This 8-pound, 10-ounce gift from God gave everyone a reason to press forward in seeking God, searching for answers to this unthinkable tragedy. This child had been born on purpose, in God's perfect, though immensely painful, timing.

As I observed the aftermath of this tragedy from halfway across the country, it was remarkable to see the countless ways in which God was at work. As new residents of the sparsely populated country town of Crook, Colorado (population 300), Kristan and Chad were unsure of where to have a funeral service for their son. A few weeks earlier they had attended a church once for Easter, so they went to talk with that pastor.

In God's inscrutable wisdom, the pastor of this tiny church in this tiny town had lost his own firstborn son many years prior in a tractor accident when he was right around Brady's age. The pastor readily agreed to host Brady's service. He became a much-needed counselor to a grieving family.

Another dilemma the heartbroken parents faced was where to bury their young son's body. There was a small family burial ground on their own ranch land where they wished to bury him, but without knowing how to get permission to do so, they began looking at cemeteries in a larger city about a half-hour away. Meanwhile, our mom was in that same larger town getting her husband's suit dry-cleaned for the funeral service. She ended up sharing with the dry cleaner that the suit was needed for a funeral. The elderly gentleman asked if the funeral was for "that little boy out in Crook." When she responded, "Yes," he asked if the family would like to bury that little boy in that cemetery on their farm.

As it turned out, that very cemetery was that dry cleaner's family plot. Yes, you read that right. It was his family's plot. This gracious gentleman quickly pulled together the permissions necessary for Brady to be buried there and one more item was checked off a pain-riddled "to do" list.

After Brady's death, Kristan and Chad began attending that little church in Crook. My sister shared with me how amazed she was that every sermon seemed to be written just for her. Rather than giving way to feelings of doubt and anger with God, she began seeking Him all the more earnestly. Kristan continued reading the Bible I had given her back in February. One day she felt compelled to look in the book of Matthew, because of her newborn son's name. Specifically, she wanted to see what chapter 5, verse 4 said, because Matthew had been born on May 4th …the 5th month on the 4th day. May 4 = 5 / 4 = Matthew 5:4.

As preposterous as this might sound, God had a message in

His living and active Word for this brokenhearted, seeking mother. Matthew 5:4 reads, "Blessed are those who mourn, for they shall be comforted." Matthew, that precious little gift from God, had indeed been born on precisely the right day.

God had known the number of Brady's days. They had been written in His book before one of them had come to be (Psalm 139:16). Matthew had been created in God's perfect timing to arrive on just the right day in the great span of time and eternity.

Do you call this a coincidence? Chance? A lucky break?

I call it, God's providence.

I call it, God's grace.

I call it, love.

Later that year, my sister committed her life to Jesus as her own Lord and Savior. This is certainly one of many times in my life when I have witnessed God working all things together for good for those who are called according to His purpose (Romans 8:28). I rejoiced that out of such unspeakable tragedy, God had born great fruit.

Brady's death impacted not only my sister and her husband. His passing caused me to

My daughter, Emily, loves
her cousin, Matthew

40

evaluate my own faith. This cascade of events grew my own faith immeasurably.

In Job 42:5, Job said to God, "I had heard of You by the hearing of the ear, but now my eye sees You." Since becoming a follower of Christ three years earlier, I'd been reading about God and hearing about God. But now I was seeing God work before my own eyes. My faith was growing in the "assurance of things hoped for, the conviction of things not seen," like Hebrews 11:1 says. God was becoming real and alive and involved in my life in a way He hadn't been before. My eyes were being more fully opened to God at work. I was seeing the incredible deeds of the Lord for myself.

Jesus had indeed become my Savior and Lord in April of 1994, but I had still largely been living day-to-day as my ol' rule-following self. I was still striving to make myself acceptable to God through obeying a set of rules. Now I was submitting to God's rules, rather than the rules that I had made up for myself, but nonetheless, I realized now that I was not daily coming to God by faith.

Somehow seeing God work so miraculously in this tragedy, I was finally beginning to grasp the Biblical truth that it was by faith, rather than by deeds, that I was made righteous. (For more on this, please read Romans, chapter 4 and Galatians, chapter 3.)

Maybe some of you are like my first self: skeptics, God-haters, and blasphemers.

Maybe some of you are like my second self: rule-followers

and law-keepers, trying to earn God's favor.

I pray that you will have the faith necessary to believe that God is really real, and that God will fill your heart and mind when you seek Him. I pray that you would be blessed with a poor, broken, meek, hungry, merciful, pure, peacemaking heart and place all your trust in the Lord alone for salvation.

A Time to Reflect

- How has God used a great tragedy in your life or someone else's life to grow your faith? How did you see God working in the midst of it?

- Read Matthew 5:1-9 in the Bible (or in the back of this book). Reflect on Jesus' declaration of the Beatitudes. Write out the verses you'd like to remember.

- When have you seen God's timing and providence? Did you deny it or receive it?

- How has God comforted you when you have mourned?

- Are you coming to God by keeping the rules, or by walking by faith? How?

Numbered Days

Sixteen months after Brady's untimely death, a white-coated doctor spoke to me across a gray, metal desk. "Mrs. Endraske, you have three options. You can terminate your pregnancy; you can do nothing and your son will die shortly after birth because his lungs will be unable to develop; or we can attempt an in-utero procedure to bypass his bladder obstruction."

Resolutely, I replied, "I'm sorry, doctor, but termination is not an option for us. We will not end this baby's life. Please, I can't imagine going through the next six months waiting for the day my son will die. Tell me more about our surgical options." The beginning of a host of questions tumbled out, "What can you do for him? Can you save him? What are the risks involved to him … and to me?"

Patiently, the maternal-fetal specialist produced a blank piece of plain, white typing paper. With a simple ballpoint pen, he began to outline our surgical options. As I understood it, I once again had three options. The doctors could use a laser to open a tiny hole in the end of our unborn son's urethra, burning out the obstruction; or they could insert a shunt to drain his bladder out the side of his belly and into the amniotic sac, bypassing the obstruction; or they could wait until further along in the pregnancy when he would be bigger, then they would remove him from my womb, surgically correct the obstruction and put him back in, where he would hopefully remain safely for the rest of the pregnancy.

Nine days earlier, during a routine ultrasound, my ob-gyn had detected my unborn son's greatly enlarged bladder. It loomed like a filled-to-burst balloon overwhelming the ultrasound screen. His enormous bladder was already as big as his small head.

Only fourteen weeks into my pregnancy, I was barely beginning to show. How could I possibly be facing these kinds of decisions? What had happened to my dream of two perfect children exactly three years apart? Why was this happening to me?

One week after our first appointment with the maternal-fetal specialist, my son's condition (which they suspected to be "posterior urethral valves") had continued to worsen to the point that the doctor feared he didn't have much time left. The operation could not wait any longer. Our son's heart appeared to be beginning to fail as a result of his still growing bladder.

On the way to the hospital for surgery, I prayed to a God who cares, that He would either completely heal our son (whom we had named Tommy), or take him quickly. The thought of carrying him for another 5 ½ months, awaiting his impending death was painful beyond comprehension.

Using an ultrasound machine to guide the instruments that the doctors inserted through two miniscule incisions in my abdomen, they attempted to insert a stent laparoscopically into the side of Tommy's bladder, so that it could drain. They were unsuccessful. Our baby boy was still so small. His position in my womb made it impossible to insert the stent. And he was too small to use the laser option. After turning off the ultrasound machine, the disappointed physician asked me to return on Monday so he could "check to see if his heart was still beating."

Following the longest weekend of my life, I learned that my son had indeed passed away. I was sent home with a prescription for pills to induce labor, a pair of clear latex gloves, and a small plastic container with a screw-on lid in which to place his remains should he be delivered at home.

On September 15, 1998, at 3:35 a.m., in a quiet, dark hospital room, Thomas William Endraske slipped silently into this world. His ten 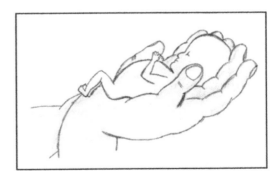 perfectly formed fingers and ten tiny toes, his two itty-bitty ears and one teeny-tiny nose, were dwarfed by his bloated belly.

Where was all the excitement that was supposed to surround the birth of a child? Where were all the eager visitors?

Twelve hours later, I was wheeled out to an awaiting car with empty arms, asking God to give me to words to explain to two-year-old Emily that her baby brother had died. I couldn't believe it. The rollercoaster that I'd hated riding had stopped, but I didn't want to get off. God had not healed my son and I fiercely grieved the loss of this much-wanted child. Crying myself to sleep night after night, my face smashed in my pillow, murmuring, "This is not what I wanted. This is not what I wanted."

While I floundered nose-deep in grief, my husband grew distant. Bill was not experiencing the profound feelings of loss that I was. Our marriage suffered as he struggled to understand my pain. I struck out at him in rage, astounded at his lack of emotion. I escaped through online forums for grieving parents; Bill escaped through TV sports and surfing the web late into the night.

Week after week, I cried out to God, begging him to heal my broken heart, and with time, He did. He comforted me in the still of the night as tears streamed down my face. I tried hard to remember that the same God who worked good in Brady's life and death, would work good in Tommy's. It was like a poem I read once about a blanket, woven from so many intricate threads and colors that we see from the underneath as only a mess of stitches while God is able to see the finished masterful design.

In the months and years that followed, I felt God propelling me to use this grief to bring Him glory. I began a ministry at my church called "A Child of Promise" to support other families continuing their pregnancy after a poor prognosis for their unborn baby.

Yet, God's relentless love did not let me stop there. Through the power of His written Word, God was transforming this one-time outspoken atheist from a floundering follower of Christ into a well-equipped Christian. I began searching the Scriptures in earnest, reading about Job's response to the loss of his own children in Job 1:20-21, "Then Job arose and tore his robe and shaved his head and fell on the ground and worshiped. And he said, "Naked I came from my mother's womb, and naked shall I return. The LORD gave, and the LORD has taken away; blessed be the name of the LORD.""

I discovered David's song in Psalm 139:13-16, "For you formed my inward parts; you knitted me together in my mother's womb. I praise you, for I am fearfully and wonderfully made. Wonderful are your works; my soul knows it very well. My frame was not hidden from you, when I was being made in secret, intricately woven in the depths of the earth. Your eyes saw my unformed substance; in your book were written, every one of them, the days that were formed for me, when as yet there was none of them."

Remembering what comfort I'd found in connecting with others online, I searched the Scriptures for words of comfort, truth, hope and peace for others who were making the difficult choice to continue their pregnancy, regardless of the severity of their child's diagnosis. I began writing a devotional guide, a companion for the lonely days, weeks and months that parents spend waiting for the arrival of their baby.

A Child of Promise: A Bible Study for Parents Facing a Poor or Fatal Prognosis for their Unborn Child was published in 2014. With lessons broken up by stages of pregnancy, parents are given journaling prompts as well as excerpts from my own story and passages of Scripture to study. From the initial excitement of finding out you are expecting; to the tests, questions and decisions faced; to the rollercoaster of waiting for the child's arrival and looking toward an uncertain future, the reader is encouraged that they are not alone.

Once again the Almighty God had brought triumph out of tragedy and beauty out of ashes.

A Time to Reflect

- Think of a time when God did not answer your prayer as you hoped. What happened? How did that feel?

- When have you seen God bring beauty from ashes?

- Read 2 Samuel 12:1-25 in the Bible (or in the back of this book). Reflect on David's experience losing his son. Then read Psalm 139:4-17 in the Bible (or in the back of this book). This psalm was written by David. Write out the verses you'd like to remember.

- What challenges are you facing right now that you need God to transform for good?

Adopted

After Tommy's death, I found myself in a peculiar place. None of my family or friends could relate to what I was going through. To them, I'd just suffered a miscarriage. In their way of thinking, of course I was sad, but this was nothing too earth shattering. They expected that I'd get pregnant again and move on down the yellow brick road toward Oz.

Even though I desperately wanted another baby, I couldn't bear the thought of going through another pregnancy. What if we lost that baby, too? I simply wasn't ready to lose another child. I found myself in a depression that I couldn't get seem to muddle my way out of on my own. I started seeing a counselor and taking anti-depressant medication.

Looking back now, I can see so many ways that I was placing my trust in my own human wisdom and fleshly desires, rather than simply trusting in my loving, Almighty God. Once again I was taking matters into my own hands, rather than leaving them in His. And God was once again working this pain out for my good and His glory.

Before Bill and I married, we had discussed having two biological children and then completing our family through adoption. So ... here we were. The way I saw it, we'd had our two biological children and now it was time for us to adopt.

The day after Tommy's due date passed, we filed our first piece of paperwork to begin what we expected to be a laborious, drawn-out process to bring our next child home. We hoped that by the following summer we would have a baby brother for our almost three-year-old daughter, Emily. To our utter disbelief, three months later, we received an unexpected phone call. There was a baby boy in Russia waiting for us to adopt. We were supposed to fly out in three weeks!

What? Huh? Three weeks you say? We're not ready! This was way too fast! Pregnancies last nine months for a reason!

I'd been calmly going through life minding my own business in the "this-might-not-work-out" stage of adoption, (or in a regular pregnancy, the "this-might-end-in-miscarraige-so-don't-get-too-excited-or-tell-too-many-people" phase) when suddenly I'd been dumped straight into the "this-baby-is-coming-right-now-and-you-better-get-to-the-hospital" stage! With hearts full of unspeakable joy, with plenty of confusion and uncertainty mixed in for good measure, we flew halfway around the world to meet the gorgeous little boy who one quick month later became our forever son. Despite my insistence that this was happening way too fast, God was once again right on time. Looking back, I can see ample evidence that confirmed God's hand of blessing on our adoption.

Our son was born the very week that Bill and I began praying to adopt a baby. The first week of January, 1999, I started keeping a journal, recording our efforts and emotions of wishing for this new family member. It sends shivers up my arms to read my journal entries for an "unnamed baby."

This black-haired, black-eyed baby boy became available for adoption the very day we arrived in Russia. (No wonder God had opened those doors so quickly for us!) He shared the same birthday as Bill's dad, which is also the day the Russian Orthodox

 church celebrates Christmas. At big sister Emily's request, we had named this never-before-met son "Nicholas" and here he was: a Christmas baby. God impressed on us again and again that we can trust His perfect timing. God is rarely early, but *never* late!

Our new son had been named Pyotr (the Russian version of Peter), a name we had considered for a middle name after my dad's nickname, "Pete." We ended up giving him Peter for his middle name. Shortly before leaving the orphanage, the orphanage director offered to get our son's baptism certificate, as well as the small plastic cross he had worn when he was baptized. Once again, I was reminded that God had a special purpose for this special little one. This precious child, born halfway around the globe, had been uniquely chosen by an all-knowing, all-seeing, merciful, gracious God, to be our "little man."

Our incredible God, whose ways are so not our own, was using this flawed mommy and this painful journey to accomplish His always-good purposes to bless both a needy orphaned boy and a needy family. But, I must confess to you that this painting that God was presenting to us was not all sunshiny yellow and bright-sky blue. There were plenty of stormy blues and melancholy greys, filling our skies and seas. In spite of my great desire for a son, my broken heart was not immediately healed by this precious little boy as I'd hoped. I struggled to love this non-stop bundle of energy who even in his short six months of life had plenty of brokenness of his own.

I thought that adopting a baby boy would "make it all better." It didn't.

Without a doubt, God had indeed brought Nick into my life for both of our good, but this child of mine was never intended to be the healer my heart. That's God's job. I was looking for a "quick fix," but there was no quick fix to be found.

I wish that I could tell you that life with an adopted son has been easy, but it hasn't. He and I have both struggled to love and accept one another. Even though Nick had been adopted as an infant, there was still pain and trauma involved. That's the truth. Yet, what is just as true, is that I would do it all again. Every single bit of pain has been worth it. I wonder what blessings have I missed out on in my efforts to avoid pain? So often, the pathway to great blessing is great struggle. Through the adoption of my son, I have learned about the unmerited, undeserved, unearned love that God has toward me. I have first-hand understanding of the Biblical concept of our adoption as God's children. I know what God means when He says that He loved me while I was still a sinner running headlong away from His love, like I never could've grasped without having this chosen child. And I love, value and treasure this incredible young man as a precious gift from a good, good, Father.

A Time to Reflect

- Has your family been blessed with the gift of a child through birth or adoption? How did you see God's providence working through that process and that child?

- Read Exodus 1:22-2:10 in the Bible (or in the back of this book). Reflect on the circumstances of Moses' adoption. Read John 1:1-13 in the Bible (or in the back of this book). Reflect on how we, too, can be adopted as children of God. Write out the verses you'd like to remember.

- How has God demonstrated His faithfulness to you in a time when you were being faithless, trusting in your own human emotions and wisdom?

- How has God blessed you as a result of a time of trial?

House Building

Two years after bringing Nick home, I started wishing for another baby. The Lord had healed my heart and I felt ready for another pregnancy, even if this baby didn't make it. I strongly believed that carrying another child would be part of the healing process for me. Bill, on the other hand, was content with the two children we had. We'd decided that I would quit my job, so I could homeschool Emily. Bill thought my hands were full … and he was right!

Once again, I began to pray, this time specifically asking for the Lord to either bless us with another child or to close my womb. And again, God answered my prayer, but not in the way I was hoping.

After a pap smear came back with evidence of precancerous cells, I underwent a high-tech procedure to remove them from my cervix. I was unaware that a rare complication of this procedure is a condition called, 'cervical stenosis,' in which the cervix heals shut. Month after month, I took pregnancy tests, shocked that I wasn't pregnant because I wasn't having a period. God, literally, had closed my womb. After six months of not having a menstrual cycle, I finally went in to my ob-gyn who performed a second LEEP procedure to surgically reopen my cervix.

The following month I found myself lying alone in our queen-sized bed, curled up in a fetal position, praying through the excruciating pain as my cervix tried to open for my monthly cycle, yet was unable to. It had happened again.

"Please, Lord, please," I cried out over and over again, trusting that God heard and saw me. Suddenly overwhelmed with both physical and emotional peace, my cervix opened and my cycle began for the first time in over half of a year.

As my grateful heart leapt within me, I found myself right back in the same dilemma. My husband was still not interested in having more children and I was. What did God want me to do now? What was He doing here? Where was His sovereign, loving, merciful hand now? Children are a blessing from the Lord, right?

O, ye of little faith. Why did I still continue to doubt God's perfect timing after seeing Him work time after time?

Gradually my prayers began to change. I started praying for God to change Bill's heart if it was His will for us to have another baby. I still did not want to get pregnant against Bill's wishes. Once again, our faithful Lord heard my cry and answered in a way I never expected. In His mysterious sovereignty, He brought a precious newborn girl in need of short-term foster care into our lives. Mackenzie Love was only with us for one week while the paperwork was completed to finalize her adoption by another family. Incredibly, her adoptive parents were friends and fellow church members with Bill's sister, Lori. For months, Lori had been praying for this family and here was their daughter, in our home! Our faithful God used Mackenzie's time in our home to give Bill a hunger to add to our family. It was amazing to see Bill's heart change seemingly overnight.

After two years of waiting and praying for another child, the Lord graciously blessed me with another beautiful daughter, Noelle Grace, our second Christmas baby. My heart swelled with unspeakable joy as I held this long awaited gift in my arms.

Because of the five-year gap between Nick and Noelle, I have frequently been asked if she was a "surprise." I love to joyfully respond, "Yes, but not how you think," and share with them the many years of praying and waiting. She certainly was a surprise

after a dozen negative pregnancy tests, but she was most definitely *not* an "accident." This Christmas blessing was and is an answer to prayer, a gift to us as I sought and trusted in a faithful God.

When Noelle was about two years old, I started praying for another child. With a five-year age gap, between our "little man" and our "princess baby," I thought it would be good for Noelle to have a sibling close to her age. Yet, once again, Bill was content with the three children we had. This time I resolved to wait on God's timing and trust that He would work this all for His glory and my good.

Shortly before Noelle's third birthday, my mom called me to share that my grandmother, who was in hospice care, was not doing well. My mom didn't think Grandma would make it much longer. I desperately wanted to see her one last time before she passed away. On the morning of December 12, 2006, I began the long drive to the northwest corner of Iowa -- unaware that God that very day had blessed me with the tiny seed of a new baby and that my sweet grandmother would pass away before I arrived.

My older sister, Kristan, discovered she was pregnant just three weeks after me and we enjoyed the fun of once again sharing our pregnancies. My extended family rejoiced at the sight of both my sister and my protruding bellies at our grandmother's memorial service, held the following summer.

My youngest son, Daniel William Endraske, was born September 2, 2007, and our family was complete (for now, at least).

A Time to Reflect

- Read Psalm 127 in the Bible (or in the back of this book). Reflect on how the Lord designed our houses to be built. Write out the verses you'd like to remember.

- How are you building your house in your own strength?

- How is the Lord building it?

- When have you waited on the Lord and He has blessed you? Was it in the way you expected?

Story Tellers

Growing up, my mom was very involved in maintaining the history and genealogy of her mother's rich Welsh heritage. The descendants of Hugh Hughes have a thick book filled with names and birthdays, anniversary dates and passing dates, as well as snippets of stories and heirloom photos, from the lives of our ancestors. Reading through it, I see the rich Christian heritage of my forefathers and I thank God for His faithfulness to the faithless.

Time, indeed, passes so quickly. Where has the time gone? As my own children have grown, I've become more and more aware of how fast time flies. When my kids were little, older women repeatedly reminded me to enjoy them, which at the time seemed impossible.

I'm beginning now to understand what they were saying, trying to soak in every minute I have with my ever-growing children (at this moment 23, 21, 15 and 11), because I know that all too soon they'll be out from under my roof. I see the value of Deuteronomy 6:7 where we are urged to teach the Lord's commandments diligently to our children, talking of them when we sit in our house, or walk by the way, or lie down, or rise up.

Under the Lord's guidance, I have tried to faithfully train my young disciples in the commands of the Scriptures, but I fear that I have failed to share as diligently with them the *stories* of the Scriptures, as well as the stories of how the Lord has worked in our own family's lives to show His power and love. While I've focused on teaching my children about God's commands, I've too often skipped over His wondrous ways.

Both the Old and New Testament are filled with stories that effectively teach us who God is by sharing with us *real* stories of *real* people being led and rescued and changed by a *real* God. And now God gives us the extraordinary opportunity to be His story tellers in our world around us, testifying of God's ongoing work in our lives, as well as testifying to the finished work of Jesus Christ through His death on the cross for our sins.

In Exodus 13, the Lord ordained the observance of the Passover, commanding for unleavened bread to be eaten for seven days followed by a celebratory feast. This annual time of remembrance was to be a fixed season for the Israelites to celebrate their deliverance from slavery in Egypt. The Lord knew that in the days to come the children would ask, "What does this mean?" thus giving parents an opportunity for generations to come to share how the Lord had rescued them.

Throughout the Scriptures, parents are commanded to pass on the truths of God's mighty works, so that the next generation will know that our Creator God is the one and only real, true, all-powerful God. But in 21st century America, most children have their eyes fixed on glowing screens, and hurried parents have their eyes fixed on upward mobility, to the neglect of this generational vision and opportunity. We have abandoned our responsibility to pass on to the next generation the stories of redemption in the Scriptures, as well the stories of how God has worked for deliverance in our own families. All too many children today (both those in our churches and those outside of them) are like the generation spoken of in Judges 2:10, "They do not know the mighty things that God has done."

Not only are parents overlooking their opportunity to pass on these stories to the next generation, we as the body of Christ are failing to share how God is working in our lives with our brothers and sisters in the faith. Despite the abundance of Facebook posts and selfie photos, we are less intimately connected than ever. Rather than sharing how God has showed up mightily to deliver us from the trappings of sin, we are sharing videos of adorable kittens and recipes of decadent pies. We have forgotten David's words in Psalm 22:22, "I will tell of your name to my brothers; in the midst of the congregation I will praise you."

I hope that this book might encourage and equip you to share the stories of your life and of the scriptures. The more you know them, the more likely you are to share them. And the more you recognize the need for others to hear what you have to say, the more likely you are to say it. Just like I would spend time memorizing a Bible verse so I can meditate on it in my quiet moments, I have memorized a brief gospel story that uses my testimony to share the good news. This way I am always prepared to share any time, any place and with any one as the Lord directs.

It goes something like this: "When I was younger, I didn't believe that God was real and my life was without purpose and hope. But when I was 21 years old, I understood for the first time, that Jesus Christ was God's own Son, that He had come to earth and lived a perfect and sinless life, performing many miracles to prove to everyone that He really was God in human flesh. The Bible tells us that, "The wages of sin is death, but the free gift of God is eternal life in Jesus Christ our Lord." I realized that my sin deserved punishment, but that Jesus had paid for those sins by His death on the cross. After being dead and buried for three days, Jesus rose from the dead, showing again that He truly was God on earth, having power over sin and death. Now Jesus is the living King and He invited us to put our trust in Him for forgiveness and everlasting life. My life has never been the same since I

72

trusted in Jesus to save me. My life has purpose and hope because of what Jesus did for me. Has anything like this ever happened to you?"

If the situation lends itself, I love to draw a little picture while I'm talking. After we're done, I can give them the picture to keep. You can share your own story of how God changed your life. Has God rescued you from slavery to pornography or drugs? Has God freed you from a critical spirit and a lying tongue? Has God changed you from a blaspheming scoffer to an outspoken believer? If you've been brought from darkness to light, God has given you a story to tell. If you're interested, you can watch a video of me sharing a diagram like this one on my YouTube channel at www.YouTube.com/formeratheist58.

So, next time you're waiting in line at the grocery store or sitting around the family dinner table, try kicking off a conversation with one way you've seen God at work in your life. Try including a simple telling of the gospel story through your own story of faith, or share how God has helped you this week to fight the good fight of faith. Start praying today for God to send people into your life who need to hear the good news of the gospel of Jesus Christ. God loves to answer those kinds of prayers.

A Time to
Reflect

- Read Psalm 78:1-8 and Psalm 145:1-12, 21 in the Bible (or in the back of this book). Reflect on God's plan for using His people as His story tellers. Write out the verses you'd like to remember.

- How did the stories you heard from your parents shape your life and faith, for better and for worse?

- How has God used you as His story teller in the past ten years? How about in the past week?

- In what ways is it easier for you to share yummy new recipes and cute cat videos than to share how God is at work in your life?

Eyewitnesses

In my family, both my father and my grandfather were lawyers. Even my mom eventually became a legal assistant, working for my dad. Growing up, our family's dinner conversations frequently revolved around whatever case my parents were working on that week. One of my first jobs was as a secretary at my dad's law office, typing briefs for my dad and his law partner. In middle school and high school, my "sports of choice" were mock trial and debate. So, when I read the word "witness" in the Bible, it stands out to me more than it might to another person.

Some of Jesus' final words before ascending to Heaven were to charge His followers with being witnesses for Him. In Acts 1:8, Jesus is recorded as saying, "But you will receive power when the Holy Spirit has come upon you, and you will be my witnesses in Jerusalem and in all Judea and Samaria, and to the end of the earth." Have you ever considered what this charge means for Christians today?

According to 1 Corinthians 15:6, over 500 men witnessed the resurrected Christ with their own eyes. But, what about us in the 21st century? None of us (me included!) have seen the risen Jesus with our own eyes or placed our fingers in His wounded side, as the disciple Thomas demanded in John 20:25. As those who have been blessed to have *not* seen and yet believed (John 20:29), how can we be eyewitnesses?

Today we are called to share our testimonies as witnesses of what we have experienced in our own lives, as well as what we have learned from studying God's Word. We ought to be compelled by the love of Christ to share our testimonies. We need to recognize how critically important the gospel story is to those living all around us. As followers of Jesus, we have been granted eternal life, yet we have been left here on earth for a purpose, to do the good works that God has prepared in advance for us to do (Ephesians 2:10). I pray that we would use our time on earth to be His "eyewitnesses."

Dictionary.com defines a witness as "an individual who, being present, personally sees or perceives a thing; a beholder, spectator, or eyewitness," "a person or thing that affords evidence," or "a person who gives testimony, as in a court of law." Going along with these three definitions of a witness, there are *two* primary requirements to being called a witness in court. A legal witness has to (1) see or perceive something and (2) tell someone. *A witness has to see or perceive something* and *tell someone*. If you don't see anything, you're not a witness, and, if you don't tell anyone what you saw, you're really not being a witness either. I call this the "seeing and telling" principle. God wants us to both SEE and TELL.

"Behold" (often translated as "look here" or "see this" in other Bible translations) appears in 1,275 different verses in the King James Bible. God *wants* us to see Him. God is not dead. God is *real* and He is alive. He calls us to notice Him.

Yet, we can't stop there. We have to follow through as God's witnesses by "bearing witness," speaking the truth in love to those around us.

It reminds me of the Samaritan woman at the well in John 4. After talking with Jesus, she "left her water jar and went away into town and said to the people, "Come, see a man who told me all that I ever did. Can this be the Christ?" (John 4:28-29) Upon hearing her testimony, many of the Samaritans believed in Jesus. Many also went to Him and asked Him to stay longer, to which Jesus stayed two additional days. And then, "many more believed because of his word. They said to the woman, 'It is no longer because of what you said that we believe, for we have heard for ourselves and we know that this is indeed the Savior of the world.'" (John 4:41-42)

This is how I hope it might be for us as witnesses for Christ. May we be a sweet aroma here on earth, sharing the truths of the gospel from the Scriptures and from our lives. And may those who hear our testimony seek out Christ for themselves, no longer believing simply because of what we said, but because they indeed meet Jesus, the Savior of the world, themselves.

Have you ever been an eyewitness to a crime? Maybe you watched a car speed through a red light and crash into another vehicle, or you witnessed a woman's purse being stolen? What did you do? What *should* you have done?

As witnesses to God's many mighty works, we bear a personal responsibility to share our eyewitness testimonies. Leviticus 5:1 tells us, "If anyone sins in that he hears a public adjuration to testify, and though he is a witness, whether he has seen or come to know the matter, *yet does not speak*, he shall bear his iniquity." As followers of Jesus Christ, our personal testimony must be seen as just as important as any court testimony. God is calling us to testify. Will we heed His call?

I wonder how often Christians fail to share their faith, out of embarrassment or fear of rejection. It grieves me to recall the opportunities I may have missed over the years because of my own unwillingness to be uncomfortable for someone else's eternal well-being. Where would I be today if Bill had not been bold enough to share the gospel with me? I am so grateful that the Lord prompted me to ask him that critically important question, "What does it mean to be saved?" and that he was prepared to give me an answer.

I'd like you to think now of a time you were surprised by a fantastic hole-in-the-wall restaurant, or spotted an unbelievable deal at your neighborhood grocery store. Did you by any chance call your best friend to tell him (or her) about it? Did you post about it on Facebook? As Richard D. Phillips wrote in his book, Jesus, the Evangelist, "If you have a good doctor, you tell your friends that they should see him when they are sick. Are your friends not sick in their souls? If you find a store with a great sale, you call your family members and friends to let them know. But here are blessings that money cannot buy – blessings that are, in fact, available to all by God's free gift of grace – and that never perish or fade."

As much as I encourage you to be a witness to those who don't know Christ, I also encourage you to be a witness to your Christian brothers and sisters. We all need the hope and joy that comes from hearing the incredible ways that God is at work all around us. Over the years I've heard some amazing stories from international missionaries. When I heard the remarkable story of how God used a run-of-the-mill gym teacher and his faithful wife to build a ministry for orphaned children in the middle of what was once a field of trash in Reynosa, Mexico, my faith in God grew. When I heard the breathtaking story of how God opened doors for a Hungarian believer to start a nationwide outreach within his country's public school system, I was in awe of God's bountiful providence and goodness. Are international missionaries the only ones who are seeing God at work? I need to be hearing more of these stories and I bet you do, too!

Finally, in addition to seeing and telling, we have to be living our daily lives as those who believe that God exists and that He rewards those who seek Him (Hebrews 11:6). As followers of Jesus Christ, we have been given the ability to walk by faith rather than sight (2 Corinthians 5:7), believing fully that "it is God who works in [us], both to will and to work for his good pleasure." (Philippians 2:13)

When I look at the lives of the forefathers of our faith like Abraham, Noah and Moses, and I see that Abraham offered up his own son, that Noah built an ark on dry land, and that Moses sprinkled lamb's blood on door posts, I am in awe. Do you think these men's actions are what you would call, 'good deeds?' I don't. These men were commended for their *faith*, which in turn led them to commit these actions of faith. As we're told in Romans 4:3, "Abraham believed God, and it was counted to him as righteousness." Our walk of faith must be more than just a list of do's and don'ts, and more than just a series of admirable good deeds.

God is *most* glorified as we follow Him by faith, loving Him with all our heart, soul, mind and strength, loving our neighbor as ourselves, living and moving and having our being in Him.

Now, in the words of Jesus, I charge you, "go therefore and make disciples of all nations, baptizing them in the name of the Father and of the Son and of the Holy Spirit, teaching them to observe all that [Jesus has] commanded you. And behold, [Jesus is] with you always, to the end of the age." (Matthew 28:19-20)

To God be all the glory, now and forever more.

A Time to Reflect

- Read John 4:25-30, 39-42 in the Bible (or in the back of this book). Reflect on what it means to be a witness for God. Write out the verses you'd like to remember.

- How has God used you as His witness? What was that experience like?

- When have you missed opportunities to be a witness for Him? How could that have gone differently?

- How have the testimonies of other Christ-followers shaped your life and faith?

Referenced Scripture Passages

Acts 8:26-40 ESV

"Now an angel of the Lord said to Philip, "Rise and go toward the south to the road that goes down from Jerusalem to Gaza." This is a desert place. And he rose and went. And there was an Ethiopian, a eunuch, a court official of Candace, queen of the Ethiopians, who was in charge of all her treasure. He had come to Jerusalem to worship and was returning, seated in his chariot, and he was reading the prophet Isaiah. And the Spirit said to Philip, "Go over and join this chariot." So Philip ran to him and heard him reading Isaiah the prophet and asked, "Do you understand what you are reading?" And he said, "How can I, unless someone guides me?" And he invited Philip to come up and sit with him.

Now the passage of the Scripture that he was reading was this: "Like a sheep he was led to the slaughter and like a lamb before its shearer is silent, so he opens not his mouth. In his humiliation justice was denied him. Who can describe his generation? For his life is taken away from the earth."

And the eunuch said to Philip, "About whom, I ask you, does the prophet say this, about himself or about someone else?"

Then Philip opened his mouth, and beginning with this Scripture he told him the good news about Jesus. And as they were going along the road they came to some water, and the eunuch said, "See, here is water! What prevents me from being baptized?"

And he commanded the chariot to stop, and they both went down into the water, Philip and the eunuch, and he baptized him. And when they came up out of the water, the Spirit of the Lord carried Philip away, and the eunuch saw him no more, and went on his way rejoicing. But Philip found himself at Azotus, and as he passed through he preached the gospel to all the towns until he came to Caesarea."

Acts 9:1-22 ESV

"But Saul, still breathing threats and murder against the disciples of the Lord, went to the high priest and asked him for letters to the synagogues at Damascus, so that if he found any belonging to the Way, men or women, he might bring them bound to Jerusalem. Now as he went on his way, he approached Damascus, and suddenly a light from heaven shone around him. And falling to the ground he heard a voice saying to him, "Saul, Saul, why are you persecuting me?" And he said, "Who are you, Lord?" And he said, "I am Jesus, whom you are persecuting. But rise and enter the city, and you will be told what you are to do." The men who were traveling with him stood speechless, hearing the voice but seeing no one. Saul rose from the ground, and although his eyes were opened, he saw nothing. So they led him by the hand and brought him into Damascus. And for three days he was without sight, and neither ate nor drank.

Now there was a disciple at Damascus named Ananias. The Lord said to him in a vision, "Ananias." And he said, "Here I am, Lord." And the Lord said to him, "Rise and go to the street called Straight, and at the house of Judas look for a man of Tarsus named Saul, for behold, he is praying, and he has seen in a vision a man named Ananias come in and lay his hands on him so that he might regain his sight." But Ananias answered, "Lord, I have heard from many about this man, how much evil he has done to your saints at Jerusalem. And here he has authority from the chief priests to bind all who call on your name."

But the Lord said to him, "Go, for he is a chosen instrument of mine to carry my name before the Gentiles and kings and the children of Israel. For I will show him how much he must suffer for the sake of my name." So Ananias departed and entered the house. And laying his hands on him he said, "Brother Saul, the Lord Jesus who appeared to you on the road by which you came has sent me so that you may regain your sight and be filled with the Holy Spirit." And immediately something like scales fell from his eyes, and he regained his sight. Then he rose and was baptized; and taking food, he was strengthened.

For some days he was with the disciples at Damascus. And immediately he proclaimed Jesus in the synagogues, saying, "He is the Son of God." And all who heard him were amazed and said, "Is not this the man who made havoc in Jerusalem of those who called upon this name? And has he not come here for this purpose, to bring them bound before the chief priests?" But Saul increased all the more in strength, and confounded the Jews who lived in Damascus by proving that Jesus was the Christ."

Luke 7:36-50 ESV

"One of the Pharisees asked him to eat with him, and he went into the Pharisee's house and reclined at table. And behold, a woman of the city, who was a sinner, when she learned that he was reclining at table in the Pharisee's house, brought an alabaster flask of ointment, and standing behind him at his feet, weeping, she began to wet his feet with her tears and wiped them with the hair of her head and kissed his feet and anointed them with the ointment. Now when the Pharisee who had invited him saw this, he said to himself, "If this man were a prophet, he would have known who and what sort of woman this is who is touching him, for she is a sinner." And Jesus answering said to him, "Simon, I have something to say to you." And he answered, "Say it, Teacher."

"A certain moneylender had two debtors. One owed five hundred denarii, and the other fifty. When they could not pay, he cancelled the debt of both. Now which of them will love him more?" Simon answered, "The one, I suppose, for whom he cancelled the larger debt." And he said to him, "You have judged rightly." Then turning toward the woman he said to Simon, "Do you see this woman? I entered your house; you gave me no water for my feet, but she has wet my feet with her tears and wiped them with her hair. You gave me no kiss, but from the time I came in she has not ceased to kiss my feet. You did not anoint my head with oil, but she has anointed my feet with ointment. Therefore I tell you, her sins, which are many, are forgiven--for she loved much. But he who is forgiven little, loves little." And he said to her, "Your sins are forgiven." Then those who were at table with him began to say among themselves, "Who is this, who even forgives sins?" And he said to the woman, "Your faith has saved you; go in peace.""

Matthew 5:1-9 ESV

"Seeing the crowds, he went up on the mountain, and when he sat down, his disciples came to him. And he opened his mouth and taught them, saying:

"Blessed are the poor in spirit, for theirs is the kingdom of heaven.

"Blessed are those who mourn, for they shall be comforted.

"Blessed are the meek, for they shall inherit the earth.

"Blessed are those who hunger and thirst for righteousness, for they shall be satisfied.

"Blessed are the merciful, for they shall receive mercy.

"Blessed are the pure in heart, for they shall see God.

"Blessed are the peacemakers, for they shall be called sons of God."

2 Samuel 12:1-25 ESV

"And the LORD sent Nathan to David. He came to him and said to him, "There were two men in a certain city, the one rich and the other poor. The rich man had very many flocks and herds, but the poor man had nothing but one little ewe lamb, which he had bought. And he brought it up, and it grew up with him and with his children. It used to eat of his morsel and drink from his cup and lie in his arms, and it was like a daughter to him. Now there came a traveler to the rich man, and he was unwilling to take one of his own flock or herd to prepare for the guest who had come to him, but he took the poor man's lamb and prepared it for the man who had come to him." Then David's anger was greatly kindled against the man, and he said to Nathan, "As the LORD lives, the man who has done this deserves to die, and he shall restore the lamb fourfold, because he did this thing, and because he had no pity."

Nathan said to David, "You are the man! Thus says the LORD, the God of Israel, 'I anointed you king over Israel, and I delivered you out of the hand of Saul. And I gave you your master's house and your master's wives into your arms and gave you the house of Israel and of Judah. And if this were too little, I would add to you as much more. Why have you despised the word of the LORD, to do what is evil in his sight? You have struck down Uriah the

Hittite with the sword and have taken his wife to be your wife and have killed him with the sword of the Ammonites. Now therefore the sword shall never depart from your house, because you have despised me and have taken the wife of Uriah the Hittite to be your wife.' Thus says the LORD, 'Behold, I will raise up evil against you out of your own house. And I will take your wives before your eyes and give them to your neighbor, and he shall lie with your wives in the sight of this sun. For you did it secretly, but I will do this thing before all Israel and before the sun.'" David said to Nathan, "I have sinned against the LORD." And Nathan said to David, "The LORD also has put away your sin; you shall not die. Nevertheless, because by this deed you have utterly scorned the LORD, the child who is born to you shall die." Then Nathan went to his house.

And the LORD afflicted the child that Uriah's wife bore to David, and he became sick. David therefore sought God on behalf of the child. And David fasted and went in and lay all night on the ground. And the elders of his house stood beside him, to raise him from the ground, but he would not, nor did he eat food with them. On the seventh day the child died. And the servants of David were afraid to tell him that the child was dead, for they said, "Behold, while the child was yet alive, we spoke to him, and he did not listen to us. How then can we say to him the child is dead? He may do himself some harm." But when David saw that his servants were whispering together, David understood that the child was dead. And David said to his servants, "Is the child dead?" They said, "He is dead." Then David arose from the earth and washed and anointed himself and changed his clothes. And he went into the house of the LORD and worshiped. He then went to his own house. And when he asked, they set food before him, and he ate. Then his servants said to him, "What is this thing that you have done? You fasted and wept for the child while he was alive; but when the child died, you arose and ate food." He said, "While the child was still alive, I fasted and wept, for I said, 'Who knows whether the LORD will be gracious to me, that the child may live?' But now he is dead. Why should I fast? Can I bring him back again? I shall go to him, but he will not return to me."

Then David comforted his wife, Bathsheba, and went in to her and lay with her, and she bore a son, and he called his name Solomon. And the LORD loved him and sent a message by Nathan the prophet. So he called his name Jedidiah, because of the LORD."

Psalm 139:4-17 ESV

"Even before a word is on my tongue, behold, O LORD, you know it altogether.

You hem me in, behind and before, and lay your hand upon me.

Such knowledge is too wonderful for me; it is high; I cannot attain it.

Where shall I go from your Spirit?

Or where shall I flee from your presence?

If I ascend to heaven, you are there!

If I make my bed in Sheol, you are there!

If I take the wings of the morning and dwell in the uttermost parts of the sea, even there your hand shall lead me, and your right hand shall hold me.

If I say, "Surely the darkness shall cover me, and the light about me be night," even the darkness is not dark to you; the night is bright as the day, for darkness is as light with you.

For you formed my inward parts; you knitted me together in my mother's womb.

I praise you, for I am fearfully and wonderfully made.

Wonderful are your works; my soul knows it very well.

My frame was not hidden from you, when I was being made in secret, intricately woven in the depths of the earth.

Your eyes saw my unformed substance; in your book were written, every one of them, the days that were formed for me, when as yet there was none of them.

How precious to me are your thoughts, O God! How vast is the sum of them!"

Exodus 1:22-2:10 ESV

"Then Pharaoh commanded all his people, "Every son that is born to the Hebrews you shall cast into the Nile, but you shall let every daughter live."

"Now a man from the house of Levi went and took as his wife a Levite woman. The woman conceived and bore a son, and when she saw that he was a fine child, she hid him three months. When she could hide him no longer, she took for him a basket made of bulrushes and daubed it with bitumen and pitch. She put the child in it and placed it among the reeds by the river bank. And his sister stood at a distance to know what would be done to him.

Now the daughter of Pharaoh came down to bathe at the river, while her young women walked beside the river. She saw the basket among the reeds and sent her servant woman, and she took it. When she opened it, she saw the child, and behold, the baby was crying. She took pity on him and said, "This is one of the Hebrews' children."

Then his sister said to Pharaoh's daughter, "Shall I go and call you a nurse from the Hebrew women to nurse the child for you?"

And Pharaoh's daughter said to her, "Go."

So the girl went and called the child's mother. And Pharaoh's daughter said to her, "Take this child away and nurse him for me, and I will give you your wages." So the woman took the child and nursed him.

When the child grew older, she brought him to Pharaoh's daughter, and he became her son. She named him Moses, "Because," she said, "I drew him out of the water.""

John 1:1-13 ESV

"In the beginning was the Word, and the Word was with God, and the Word was God. He was in the beginning with God. All things were made through him, and without him was not any thing made that was made. In him was life, and the life was the light of men.

The light shines in the darkness, and the darkness has not overcome it.

There was a man sent from God, whose name was John. He came as a witness, to bear witness about the light, that all might believe through him. He was not the light, but came to bear witness about the light.

The true light, which gives light to everyone, was coming into the world. He was in the world, and the world was made through him, yet the world did not know him. He came to his own, and his own people did not receive him. But to all who did receive him, who believed in his name, he gave the right to become children of God, who were born, not of blood nor of the will of the flesh nor of the will of man, but of God."

Psalm 127 ESV

"A Song of Ascents. Of Solomon.

Unless the LORD builds the house, those who build it labor in vain.

Unless the LORD watches over the city, the watchman stays awake in vain.

It is in vain that you rise up early and go late to rest, eating the bread of anxious toil; for he gives to his beloved sleep.

Behold, children are a heritage from the LORD, the fruit of the womb a reward.

Like arrows in the hand of a warrior are the children of one's youth.

Blessed is the man who fills his quiver with them!

He shall not be put to shame when he speaks with his enemies in the gate."

Psalm 78:1-8 ESV

"A Maskil of Asaph. Give ear, O my people, to my teaching; incline your ears to the words of my mouth!

I will open my mouth in a parable; I will utter dark sayings from of old, things that we have heard and known, that our fathers have told us.

We will not hide them from their children, but tell to the coming generation the glorious deeds of the LORD, and his might, and the wonders that he has done.

He established a testimony in Jacob and appointed a law in Israel, which he commanded our fathers to teach to their children, that the next generation might know them, the children yet unborn, and arise and tell them to their children, so that they should set their hope in God and not forget the works of God, but keep his commandments; and that they should not be like their fathers, a stubborn and rebellious generation, a generation whose heart was not steadfast, whose spirit was not faithful to God."

Psalm 145:1-12, 21 ESV

"A Song of Praise. Of David.

I will extol you, my God and King, and bless your name forever and ever.

Every day I will bless you and praise your name forever and ever.

Great is the LORD, and greatly to be praised, and his greatness is unsearchable.

One generation shall commend your works to another, and shall declare your mighty acts.

On the glorious splendor of your majesty, and on your wondrous works, I will meditate.

They shall speak of the might of your awesome deeds, and I will declare your greatness.

They shall pour forth the fame of your abundant goodness and shall sing aloud of your righteousness.

The LORD is gracious and merciful, slow to anger and abounding in steadfast love.

The LORD is good to all, and his mercy is over all that he has made.

All your works shall give thanks to you, O LORD, and all your saints shall bless you!

They shall speak of the glory of your kingdom and tell of your power, to make known to the children of man your mighty deeds, and the glorious splendor of your kingdom....

My mouth will speak the praise of the LORD, and let all flesh bless his holy name forever and ever."

John 4:25-30, 39-42 ESV

"The woman said to him, "I know that Messiah is coming (he who is called Christ). When he comes, he will tell us all things." Jesus said to her, "I who speak to you am he."

Just then his disciples came back. They marveled that he was talking with a woman, but no one said, "What do you seek?" or, "Why are you talking with her?"

So the woman left her water jar and went away into town and said to the people, "Come, see a man who told me all that I ever did. Can this be the Christ?" They went out of the town and were coming to him. ...

Many Samaritans from that town believed in him because of the woman's testimony, "He told me all that I ever did." So when the Samaritans came to him, they asked him to stay with them, and he stayed there two days. And many more believed because of his word. They said to the woman, "It is no longer because of what you said that we believe, for we have heard for ourselves, and we know that this is indeed the Savior of the world.""

Acknowledgements

Many thanks to:

- My faithful husband, Bill, for not only sharing the truth of the gospel of Jesus Christ with me, but also for modeling His steadfast love.

- My precious children, Emily, Nick, Noelle and Daniel, for enduring with patience the countless hours I've spent working on this project.

- My mom and dad for training me to seek the truth with a diligent, inquisitive spirit.

- My sister, Kristan, for walking this journey to faith with me and for praying for me every step of the way.

- My friend and mentor, Dee, for encouraging me to have a daily time with God each and every day and to mine the Word for truth.

- My church family at Collierville Bible Church for your faithful leadership and for having an indescribably incredible women's ministry team that has taught me to love God and one another, and to passionately pursue my God-given purpose. Thanks, y'all!

Recommended Resources

- <u>More than a Carpenter</u> and <u>Evidence that Demands a Verdict</u> by Josh McDowell

- <u>The Case for Faith</u> and <u>The Case for Christ</u> by Lee Strobel

- <u>Jesus, the Evangelist</u> by Richard D. Phillips

- www.AnswersInGenesis.org

About the Author

Kim's testimony of coming out of atheism to find faith in Christ is a popular YouTube video and is featured on her FormerAtheist58 YouTube channel. This Memphis-area resident is a committed wife, homeschooling mom and gifted speaker. Kim is the author of "A Child of Promise," which weaves her story of continuing her pregnancy following an adverse prenatal diagnosis with Scripture and journaling prompts. She is also the founder of an online support ministry by the same name. www.achildofpromise.org

Follow her at www.teachwhatisgood.com, as well as Facebook and Instagram.

"You have multiplied, O LORD my God,
your wondrous deeds and your thoughts toward us;
none can compare with you!
I will proclaim and tell of them,
yet they are more than can be told....
I have told the glad news of deliverance
in the great congregation;
behold, I have not restrained my lips,
as you know, O LORD.
I have not hidden your deliverance within my heart;
I have spoken of your faithfulness and your salvation;
I have not concealed your steadfast love
and your faithfulness from the great congregation."

Psalm 40:5, 9-10

Made in the USA
Columbia, SC
22 September 2025

70013160R00072